WHAT IF GODZILLA JUST WANTED A HUG?

Leading with the Heart Instead of the Chin

Written and Illustrated by
DARRELL FUSARO

www.ThisWillMakeYouHappy.com

www.ThisWillMakeYouHappy.com

First Printing, 2013

ISBN 978-1493627998

GOD LIKES YOU!

CONTENTS

ACKNOWLEDGEMENT

This book is not entirely my fault. Others who deserve blame include Mike Dugan for helping me develop a healthy perspective on life and my wife Lori for encouraging me whenever I lose that healthy perspective. There's graphic designer Tiffany Yang for assisting me in creating a framework that enabled me to proceed with arranging all my miscellaneous drawings, sketches, notes and stories into a legitimate-looking book. I must also point out Kathy Carroll and Cassie Craig who, after reading my rough drafts, cared enough to risk our life-long friendship by taking the time to highlight flaws, errors, and incomprehensible writing. If you're a friend or family member and feel slighted that I haven't mentioned you by name, please know in some way you're to blame as well.

Off to make a
good impression!

IT'S NOT WHAT YOU THINK OF ME THAT MAKES ME UPSET, IT'S WHAT I THINK YOU THINK OF ME THAT MAKES ME UPSET

Personally, I enjoy my Italian last name. Fusaro. Some say "Foo-SAH-row" while others say "Fuzz-AH-row." Even I go back and forth. Maybe if I were less American and more Italian, I'd know right from wrong. But either way, I like it. The problem is the lethal combination of 'Darrell' and 'Fusaro.' Some things just don't go together, and my first and last name are a perfect example. Together there's no punch. Darrell Fusaro sounds too rhymie and weak. Maybe it's in the pronunciation? In New Jersey, where I grew up, Darrell is pronounced, 'Daaaah-rel.' I don't know. My father was James and so was my grandfather, which is a perfect compliment to Fusaro. But Darrell? What was my mother thinking?

Recently, I asked her where the name came from.

"I don't know." She said, "Funny, isn't it? I never knew of a Darrell before you were born. When you came out it just hit me. 'Darrell!' Maybe you named yourself?"

Great. With only myself to blame, I guess I have to learn to accept it, because for some strange reason the thought of changing it now seems sacrilegious.

But growing up surrounded by Tonys, Frankies, Tommys, Larrys, Mikes and Jimmys, it didn't feel good to be a Darrell. Today there is a bright side. Old friends and acquaintances have no problem finding me. I'm the only Darrell Fusaro on Facebook. I would love to tell you I am the only Darrell Fusaro in the world, but that's not the case. If you Google "Darrell Fusaro," you will discover there is one other, who is also American and approximately the same age. But that's where the similarities end. The other Darrell Fusaro is a martial arts champion living in Minnesota. That Darrell Fusaro is probably calm, confident, and armed only with a paper clip, I imagine able to defend himself against eighteen men. Me? I'm the guy who after starting an argument with someone bigger than me will mimic a karate stance I saw on an episode of the TV show, *Kung-Fu*, shout "Hi-yah!" at the top of my lungs and then turn and run for my life.

So at least in name, I'm not as unique as I thought and my last name makes me even less unique since it is clearly Italian. This puts me into a large and well-known nationality. Most Italian-Italians, the ones from Italy, always seem to be curious as to how we Italian-Americans are perceived by others in America. With all the news they've heard of Italian stereotypes in America, like the ones put forward in "The Godfather," "The Sopranos," "Mafia Wars," and "The Jersey Shore," I understand

8

what they expect. However, once people discover-er I'm Italian, their reaction is always the same. It goes like this: "Wow, you're Italian?" They seem surprised, most likely thrown off by the name Darrell. Then they exclaim, "I love Italian food!" Disappointing, isn't it? No one has ever accused me of being in the Mafia, and in spite of growing up in New Jersey and spending every summer at the Shore, I've never been considered a Guido ei-ther. Apparently, no matter what negative Italian stereotype comes down the pike it will always be overshadowed by the strength of Italy's most pow-erful and effective good will ambassador: its cui-sine. Honestly, even with Italian food as my ally, I've always been judged more by my behavior than by my name. Which is usually a good thing.

By the way, if you ever meet another Italian kid from New Jersey named "Darrell," give him my condolences.

"There is no prejudice that the work of art does not finally overcome." - Andre Gide

"What the hell did I do to deserve this?"

a short sided view of Metamorphosis

MY BIG BREAK
WAS A HUMBLE JOB IN HOLLYWOOD

Several years ago, I received a letter congratulating me on a short video documentary I produced about the doorman at the Four Seasons Hotel, NYC. It was from the Hollywood director Joel Schumacher and, in a friendly way, he said, "You are an excellent Director." Somehow this letter activated delusions of grandeur. I decided to leave New York, abandon my art career and move to Los Angeles. "Hollywood here I come!" My girlfriend, Lori, now my wife, was an actress so it was easy to convince her that this move would be great for the both of us. Within a few weeks we landed in Los Angeles.

Spotting celebrities and driving by famous locations seen on television was exciting! Soon we began to suspect familiar-looking strangers were celebrities, whispering to each other, "I think that's someone famous." But our excitement diminished as our credit card balances grew. My focus soon shifted from making it in the movies to just making it, period. What the hell was I thinking? Moving to L.A. was beginning to look like a tragic mistake. To ease my worry, I figured out if worse came to worse, we could survive if I found a job that netted just $10 an hour. So, I took immediate action, filling out two applications a day. The only requirement I had for any job was that it paid $10 an hour. As I set out each day I repeated an affirmative rhyme I read in the book, "The Game of Life and How to Play It," by Florence Scovel Shinn. It goes, "I have a wonderful job in a wonderful way, I give wonderful service for wonderful pay." This would squelch my panic and renew my faith that I would have the right job, at the right time, in the right way, if I just stayed the course. It also helped me accept the fact that even if moving to L.A. was a blunder, nothing happens by mistake, and a wonderful opportunity, if only for growth, would present itself. To be honest, I was still hoping for something better than just growth.

Then out of nowhere, a neighbor familiar with my situation came with good news. He said his mother was having a difficult time finding an artist for a job she had available and since I was an artist and needed a job, he thought I might be interested. My enthusiasm rose. "Nothing happens by mistake," I told myself. Maybe I was led to Los Angeles, not to work in the movies, but to kick-start my art career! I was very excited about this new possibility. He seemed glad that I was eager and went on to explain what the job would be. He said his mother needed someone with artistic ability to paint neon bulbs. "What do you mean paint neon bulbs?" I thought. He explained that the job was to dip glass neon bulbs into paint and then hang them to dry.

"What the @#*? You mean like on an assembly line?" I didn't say that out loud. The voice in my head continued, "You exhibited with Andy Warhol in New York City and now you're going to work in an L.A. sweatshop? How pathetic." But humility born out of desperation coerced me to ask, "How much?"

"Ten bucks an hour," he replied.

The next day I was alone wearing protective gloves and a mask in an abandoned airplane hangar dipping delicate glass neon bulbs in paint and carefully hanging them on fishing line to dry. Nothing could be further from my dream to be an art star or Hollywood player. But I accepted it and surrendered to the fact that this was meeting our needs. I decided to swim with the current and continued with my silly little rhyme as I dipped each bulb and hung it to dry; "I have a wonderful job in a wonderful way, I give wonderful service for wonderful pay!"

Soon I began to look forward to my days dipping the neon bulbs in paint. It became a pleasant form of meditation. I started to take pride in my daily output, striving to keep up with the load of unpainted neon bulbs that would be delivered by my neighbor's mom each day. Her name was Barbara Ryan and she always came delivering the bulbs with a smile and a compliment She'd never grew tired of letting me know how happy she was that I was willing to take the job.

After a couple of months, I had completed about a thousand bulbs when Barbara came to inform me that . . . that was it. I was done painting neon bulbs; my job was finished. For a moment I thought, "Now what will I do?" Believe it or not I really began to enjoy this humble labor.

"Can you stay on and work on the set installing them?" she asked.

Did she just say, "On the set?" Barbara explained that all the neon bulbs were for a miniature recreation of the Las Vegas strip to be used in a movie. She also went on to explain that her boss Larry Albright, was a Hollywood legend. Larry Albright? Really? That funny old man who looked like Albert Einstein? I had no idea, he just seemed like a regular guy. She filled me in on how he was responsible for many award-winning lighting effects, including those seen in, *Close Encounters*, *Star Wars* and even Michael Jackson's illuminated shirt and sidewalk featured in the classic *Billy Jean* music video.

The next day I was on the set, a small airfield in Simi Valley, CA where a crew was working on the miniature Las Vegas strip. I was shown a 1/15th scale replica of the Las Vegas Hard Rock Hotel sign still under construction. It was my responsibility to install all the neon and illuminate the sign under Larry Albright's specifications. The movie was titled, *Con Air* and all I knew about it at that time was that we were creating the miniatures for a stunt where a large model C-123 Provider plane, nicknamed the 'Jailbird,' would smash through the Hard Rock Hotel sign and crash land on the replicated Las Vegas strip. I was amazed at how real the models looked. This was even better than I imagined it would be. I reflected back to memories of my childhood fascination watching the behind the scenes making of *Star Wars* on TV. Each day was spent carefully adhering and wiring the delicate neon bulbs on the sign, all the while enthusiastically reminding myself, "I have a wonderful job in a wonderful way, I give wonderful service for wonderful pay!" In two months the sign was completed. When we lit it up for the first time, the fragrance of a fresh clean spring day started to fill the room. Apparently the power packs were emitting some sort of gas. Even though I enjoyed the fragrance, I had a hunch this may not be good to inhale. So, I decided to inform the Art Director, Mike Stuart, and ask him if he knew if the fumes were lethal.

"You would know better than me, you're the electrical engineer." He responded.

"What?" I went on to explain that, "I'm no electrical engineer, I got hired off the street to paint neon bulbs in a shed for ten bucks an hour."

"Yeah, right Fusaro," Mike said, "In any case, I was hoping you would be able to stay on and supervise the stunt."

Supervise the stunt? I felt like I was in over my head, but with the sign completed, Larry Albright's contract was over so I'd be jobless if I didn't accept Mike's offer. Once again it was intuitively obvious, "Of course I could stay on."

Within ten minutes I was signing contracts with Disney as a 'Special Effects Stunt Supervisor.' For the final weeks before and up until the actual filming of the stunt, I was on hand during the rehearsals to insure the sign would operate according to plan. When the day finally came to film the stunt, every crew member and subcontractor who had contributed to the stunt, including Larry Albright and Barbara, came to watch. At the moment the director shouted, "Action!" the model C-123 "Jailbird" smoking with engine fire FX and suspended by cables high above the airfield was released. It flew perfectly, heading directly into the illuminated Hard Rock Hotel sign. Upon contact the sign exploded into flames as six high-speed cameras caught the action. When "Cut!" was shouted the applause and cheers were spontaneous.

Six months later, sitting in a theater with Lori waiting to see *Con Air*, I realized how fortunate I was to have been offered that $10 an hour job and grateful that I didn't snub my nose at it.

ITALIAN-AMERICAN NICKNAMES
ARE NO JOKE

Everyone's familiar with nicknames.   Mikey, Snookie, Noodles, The Situation.   We've heard them all.   But it's the ones given to you by your Italian-American friends that seem to carry clout. I discovered   this while looking for work in the entertainment industry.   It happened during the time I was making calls trying to land interviews. I knew it wasn't going to be easy.   The problem is my name, "Darrell Fusaro."   Why?   Here's an example.   I dial up the number I have for an executive at a local studio.   The executive's receptionist answers, "So and so's office, how may I help you?"

With every ounce of courage I ask, "May I please speak to so and so?"

"Who may I say is calling?"

"Darrell Fusaro."

"Dale?'

"Darrell."

"Harold?"

"No, it's Darrell . . .

18

"I'm sorry, what is your last name?"

"Fusaro."

"Gerald Bizarro?"

Eventually we'd get past my name and the receptionist would promise to pass along my information. But by then my confidence would always be depleted. I knew I'd never hear back from them. Although feeling disappointed and ineffective, I plodded along and made another call. Frustrated after the dreaded "Who may I say is calling?", I blurted out my childhood nickname, "Fuzzy Fusaro." The receptionist put me on hold and within seconds there was a man's voice on the line, "Fuzzy Fusaro, what can I do for you?"

For the first time in my life, I was being treated like a "somebody." It was remarkable. Who did he think I was? Could my Italian-American nickname really make that much difference in how I am perceived? Who cares? I liked it.

Next thing I knew, I was signed with an agent named "Dick Woody." (Yeah, and I thought my name was bad). Before the ink was dry on the contract I was starring in TV commercials. At every shoot it seemed like they rolled out the red carpet for me. Dick Woody was calling me every week with another director who wanted him to "get Fuzzy!" I even got a call from Nicholas Pileggi, best known for writing the book and screenplay for the movie *Goodfellas*. What was the cause of all this new-found respect? Could it be that my silly childhood nickname was being perceived by Hollywood as that of a Mafioso? Regardless of what the cause might have been, this true Hollywood story was soon coming to an end.

The Screen Actors Guild was organizing a strike for higher wages, but Dick Woody was still getting calls for me to work. When I voiced my concern Dick Woody reassured me I had nothing to worry about. And just like in a classic Greek tragedy when the main character chooses to ignore their conscience in the pursuit of fame and fortune and knows better, their downfall is for certain. Mine was swift. Someone dropped a dime about me working on a commercial during the strike and the Screen Actors Guild called me in for questioning. Just like you'd expect in a Mob trial, I was sitting at a desk with a microphone answering questions from a panel of inquisitors. The jig was up. I got sentenced to five years. I wasn't permitted to accept a union acting gig for five full years. Dick Woody folded up shop and it was over as fast as it started.

Humbled, I retreated back to my ordinary life as Darrell Fusaro. At first I felt robbed of my chance to make it big, but once I settled down, I realized that during my rise to perceived stardom I was actually more anxious than happy. I have to be reminded of this fact, because every once in a while I still get the urge to resurface as "Fuzzy Fusaro."

ITALIANS, BLACKS, & MEXICANS;
WE ALL HAVE GRANDMAS

On February 1, 2001, I had to prove that I was Italian-American. I brought this upon myself a month earlier when I made the mistake of boasting to an acquaintance. I told her about my going to art school in New Jersey and how often I was invited by my niece's elementary school to come in and draw for the kids. So, when the acquaintance asked me if I would like to do that here in Los Angeles, I said, "Of course!" She said, "Great!" and invited me to do the same for the kids in a Head Start program located in Watts, CA. Watts! What did I just get myself into? I've seen the inner city gang movie *Colors.* I began to panic. I had nothing in common with these kids. What are they going to think about this blue-eyed devil coming into their school? The fact that they were only preschoolers didn't matter. They are going to hate me. But I didn't want to look bad, so I handed her my business card. She took one look at it and said, "You're Italian? That's great! You can tell them what it's like to be Italian-American."

You mean being white and living in the suburbs didn't set me apart enough? Then I had a brutal awakening: I'm an Italian-American? All of a sudden, it felt like the past thirty-nine years I had been masquerading as an Italian-American and now someone was calling my bluff. How am going to prove it? I'm not qualified. I am nothing like what people expect when they imagine an Italian-American. I can't speak Italian, I don't know how to play the mandolin or accordion, I'm not a tough guy or Mafioso type, I don't watch soccer, never belonged to an Italian club, the only thing Italian about me is the fact that my grandparents were from Italy. Even more embarrassing was that in spite of all the years I ate and enjoyed my grandmother's authentic Italian cooking I never bothered to learn what any of it was called. I was beginning to think that all I knew about being Italian-American was what I learned from watching TV. Then when word was out that an "authentic" Italian-American was doing a goodwill presentation for the unfortunate children of Watts, the Italian Consulate General jumped on board to host the event. What are they going to expect from me? Well, on the bright side, I didn't have to worry about going to Watts anymore. Until I got a call inviting me to visit their school. The head of the program wanted me to see how the topic of my upcoming presentation inspired the teachers, parents, and students.

When I arrived at the school I was greeted by the head of the program and she seemed genuinely happy to see me. She was an attractive African-American woman with a British accent who enthusiastically led me to the classroom. The teachers and the children were very excited to meet me. Their classroom was decorated with large pictures depicting life in Italy and construction paper maps of Italy the children had made. The children's maps had different uncooked pastas, seeds and other tiny items glued to them, representing the places these items and objects originated from. Sweet memories of my childhood began to surface. I remembered how much fun I had doing the same types of things in elementary school with my classmates. The program head went on to share how all the parents were making Italian foods at home and teaching the kids everything they knew about Italy. Wow, the people in Watts were nothing like I imagined. They were just like me. I expected to be judged and instead I got handshakes, smiles, and hugs. That's when it hit me. It was our similarities that impressed me. Recognizing our similarities made me feel included and loved, in spite our differences. Funny, when I focused on our differences, I worried, but when I focused on our similarities I felt at home. This became my inspiration. I knew one thing every kid loved was cartoons, and even more fascinating than that is watching someone draw them. So that's what I'd do. I'd tell the simple story of my grandparents traveling from Italy to America on a boat, how they started a family and from there on the rest of my story is similar to most American kids; I went to school and loved spaghetti.

I started to imagine how great it would be if I had a magic pad. A pad that magically brought to life whatever I drew on it. So that's what I set out to do. I constructed a magic pad using a large four foot roll of paper and a clothes rack. I hung the roll of paper on the horizontal bar of the clothes rack like a giant roll of toilet paper, so I would be able to pull the paper down like a window shade and draw the cartoons that illustrated my story on it. After each drawing I'd have the kids say a magic word and then I'd reach through a slit I'd make in the paper and pull out the real object that I had just drawn.

On February 1, 2001, the kids were bused from Watts to the Italian Cultural Institute located in Westwood, CA. They were all led into the theatre where my magic pad awaited on stage sleeping. It was obvious the pad was sleeping because it had a sleeping face drawn on it. At the start of the show

I apologized in advance to the audience explaining that the pad had a late night and that whenever I wake him up like this he can be uncooperative. That's when I told the kids what the magic word was. Because we didn't know what to expect from the pad, the magic word was, "Eye-Yī-Yī!" The saying "Eye-Yī-Yī" is significant for me because it's what I say to myself whenever I'm overwhelmed, and, since I picked it up from my grandfather, I assume it's Italian.

I started the show by drawing an outline of Italy. Then we all said the magic word together, and instead of pulling out a real map of Italy, I got a shiny red go-go boot instead. Holding up the boot, I said, "I guess that's close, Italy does look like a boot, doesn't it?" The kids all laughed and it went on from there, I drew a boat, and pulled out rubber ducks, on and on, one mishap after another had all the children laughing and learning. For my final drawing I had the kids help me draw a picture of my grandmother by calling out the different items our grandmothers' wear. This grandma had on a dress, with a coat to keep warm, a hat, a pair of nice shoes, glasses, a nice purse, and her hair was done perfectly, of course.

When I was done drawing Grandma, we heard a woman's voice yell out, "Mangia! Mangia!" Earlier in the show we learned "Mangia" was Italian for "Let's eat!" but where was it coming from? The kids trying to help me, all pointed to the pad. Really? From the pad? Could it be Grandma? I told the kids how special it would be for me if they could help make my grandma appear. But since the pad had been acting funny all morning, they would have to try really hard so the pad knew this was a special request. They were more than willing. So, on the count of three we all yelled the magic word, "Eye-YĪ-Yī!" Then I reached through the paper and grabbed the hand of my Grandma, played by my wife, and pulled her through the pad and on to the stage with me. She looked exactly like the grandma we drew. The kids all screamed with surprise and delight.

After the show, while everyone was being escorted into the atrium to be treated to an Italian feast, compliments of the Italian Consulate, I felt a tug on my pant leg. I turned around to see three smiling little children looking up at me, "Where's Grandma?" they asked. I brought them to where my wife, still as Grandma, was seated. Children surrounded her. They all wanted to eat their spaghetti with Grandma. Well, I may not have been the star of the show but it sure felt great to be a part of it.

When everyone left and I was packing up, the Consul General walked up to me, shook my hand enthusiastically and said, "Bravo!" Then he asked how long I had been doing my "Italian-American" presentation for kids? He said it was wonderful and asked if I'd be willing to do it again sometime. "Of course!" was my answer.

MAKERS OF MAGIC MOP INFOMERCIAL & A SHIT-FLINGING MONKEY
ARE INSULTED BY COMPARISON TO MY MOVIE

My immigrant grandparents would be proud to know that today I am living the American dream. Not only have I enjoyed the freedom of expression as granted by our First Amendment rights, I have been on the receiving end of it as well. Recently, I received some anonymous internet comments regarding my first documentary film, "The Basement." They praise my ability to have made the "worst piece of filmmaking ever!" Here are some more excerpts:

"Life is full of surprises. Sometimes you get genital herpes . . ."

"The camera work seems as if the cameraman was drunk and this so-called movie was being shot from the inside of a liquor store paper bag."

" . . . the nausea from this pile of dung made it really hard to focus."

"I'd . . . compare it to a Magic Mop infomercial and whatever movie a sh*t-flinging monkey would do, had he a $7 budget."

The last one is my all time favorite, even if the makers of the Magic Mop infomercial and a sh*t-flinging monkey are insulted by being compared to me. Unfortunately when criticism is this outrageously over-the-top, it is hard to take it seriously. I also believe the ability to remain anonymous when being critical amplifies the cruelty, as pointed out in the New York Times, April 21, 2010, article by writer Taffy Brodesser-Akner, *E-Playgrounds Can Get Vicious*. In it she writes, "Why is the Internet such a cruel playground? Kathleen Taylor, the author of *Cruelty: Human Evil and the Human Brain*, has a theory. 'We're evolved to be face-to-face creatures,' she said in a recent interview. 'We developed to have constant feedback from others, telling us if it was O.K. to be saying what we're saying. On the Internet, you get nothing, no body language, no gesture. So you get this feeling of unlimited power because there is nothing stopping you, no instant feedback."

This by no means diminished the sting of such criticism, but if I worry about what people may or may not like about every new endeavor I embark on, I'd never have the courage to start at all. One childhood experience stands out. While I was in elementary school my third grade teacher asked the class, "What year did Christopher Columbus discover America?" A rhyme I had learned rang out in my head, "In 1492, Columbus sailed the ocean blue." I knew the answer! But as I was about to raise my hand my enthusiasm was replaced with a terrifying thought. "What if that's not the right answer? Everyone will make fun of me!" So, I didn't raise my hand, and John Grimaldi did.

He answered, "1492!"

From that moment on, I despised John Grimaldi. Anytime anyone mentioned John Grimaldi, I would make comments like, "He's a brown-noser. A real apple polisher. A goody two shoes. What a weasel." I never had anything nice to say about John Grimaldi. My contempt for John Grimaldi was with me right up until I graduated from high school. Why did I hate John Grimaldi? Was it because he knew the answer? Not at all. I hated John Grimaldi because he had the courage to do what I could not. He was able to take the risk and raise his hand regardless of potential ridicule.

That being said, whenever I step out of my comfort zone and into something new, I have to be mature enough to learn from all the constructive criticism offered. If I refuse to consider the constructive criticism from those with more experience than myself, I would never improve at all. The key word here is, "constructive."

When I was serving in the Military, a U.S. Marine Corps Gunnery Sergeant asked me the following question.

"Fusaro, do you know what the biggest room in your house is?"

"The living room?" I answered.

"No you idiot, the room for improvement!"

So today I see these critiques and comments as a compliment to my ability to finally have the courage demonstrated by John Grimaldi. They also reinforce my gratitude to be living in America where we have the freedom of expression, the right to be wrong, the ability to try and fail, and the courage to learn from or ignore the criticism of others So feel free to comment.

ANYTHING WORTH DOING
IS WORTH DOING BADLY

Are you sure
this meeting is Anonymous?

Everyone loves a hero! They are living proof that dreams are attainable. We believe if they can do it, so can we. Unfortunately, for me heroes were a bummer. You see, I belong to a smaller group who instead of being inspired, are overwhelmed by the great accomplishments of others. We feel intimidated by heroes, believing that they possess a secret something we lack. So we tend to give up without ever trying. Then we wander the earth condemned to live life alternating between regret for never having tried and resentful toward those who made it. Of course we tell ourselves it was only because they got all the breaks that we really deserved, but deep down we know better.

So, how do those of us who tend to fall prey to this way of thinking find inspiration? I have found the answer, and it has become my motto for success. "Anything worth doing, is worth doing badly." Credit for this conclusion must go to one of my former art instructors at the now defunct Newark School of Fine and Industrial Arts. His name was Mr. Bonavito. He was a real old-timer rumored to have exhibited with Picasso. Ironically, this transformative event occurred the day he caught me checking out a book of Picasso's masterpieces. He peered over my shoulder to see what I was looking at and then said,

"Don't look at that, it'll screw your head up!"

I looked up at him, "Really?"

"Yes, if you want to be inspired don't compare yourself to what these guys accomplished at the height of their careers. Compare your work to what they were doing when they were just starting out. You'll see most of their stuff was crap, just like yours."

That was the most striking compliment I had ever received. Mr. Bonavito's simple advice revolutionized my outlook. It clicked! The secret to succeeding is that it's OK to suck as a beginner. For the first time in my life I realized that everyone sucked as a beginner, even Picasso; and everyone was insecure in the beginning too. Even the most courageous have insecurities about a new challenge. Maybe this should have been obvious, but I never even considered it. It's inspiring to realize that if my heroes could suck as beginners, then I could too.

So, if you are starting on a new adventure toward your heart's desire, be inspired that those you look up to were once just as insecure and inexperienced as you. Remind yourself that anything worth doing is worth doing badly and before you know it you'll be a hero motivating others with your lousy start too.

THE WORST THING THAT COULD HAPPEN
IS OFTEN THE BEST

Lori, my wife and professional photographer, had mistakenly booked a photo session that over-lapped with her commitment to lead a business meeting. What happened was, she got someone to fill for the meeting on the wrong day. Now she was stuck having to lead the meeting, she couldn't believe she made such a stupid mistake. The photo session she booked was for a two-year-old's birthday party.

When covering a child's birthday, the photographer must be on time to capture the scheduled itinerary of events, so the stress was severe. How could Lori possibly make it on time? Her business meeting was further away from the party's location than our home. In addition, the meeting was scheduled to end within minutes of the party's start. So, Lori asked if I could help out by acting as her assistant and showing up to the party on time with her second camera. This way if she was running late, I could reassure the client of Lori's arrival and, having assisted her in the past, cover the event until she arrived.

So that being the plan, Lori headed off to her meeting and I printed up directions on MapQuest. The location was just eighteen miles away from our home but just to be safe I gave myself an hour to get there. It was Sunday, the skies were blue, the sun shining, the roads were clear and I zipped onto the freeway. I turned up the radio and I was on my way to save the day for Lori. The freeway was clear as I had predicted. Traveling along at 65 mph plus, I was already enjoying the coffee I imagined I'd have more than enough time to treat myself to when I arrived. Within just ten minutes of travel time, I was already past the halfway mark. There was a curve in the freeway and then I hit a wall of traffic. No big deal, I reassured myself that I had more than enough time, I'm more than halfway there, and I am sure it'll open up soon. Ten minutes later and less than a mile traveled, I kept my cool by reassuring myself with the affirmations, nothing happens by mistake, Divine Order prevails, and I'll get there right when I am supposed to. I can do without the coffee.

Another ten minutes, still inching along and unable to see any clearing ahead, I decided to keep busy by listening to messages and returning phone calls. This kept me occupied for another ten minutes and only one more mile. Now with the party starting in ten minutes and with seven more miles to go in this traffic, I could not deny it any longer; there was no way I would be there on time. My concern began to grow into worry. I began repeating my affirmations from the preceding paragraph when it hit me. What about Lori? I hope she is not behind me in this nightmare. If she is, then she will be counting on my already being at the party. I was apprehensive to call her, afraid she would be stuck in traffic too, and probably be extremely upset with herself. If that were the case, then I knew once she heard that I wasn't going to be on time either . . . well, I'll be nice and say it wasn't going to be good for me. I held on to the desperate belief that the traffic would miraculously open up. It didn't. So, I bit the bullet and called Lori. While the phone was ringing I was rehearsing how I was going to explain that I left with over an hour ahead of the call time and that there was no accounting for this traffic.

"Hello?" she answered.

"Lori?"

"How close are you?" she asked.

I spit it out quickly, like tearing off a Band-Aid, "I'm stopped dead in traffic, still downtown . . . I think they closed off the highway."

"That's OK, I'm here already."

"What? Really? You are? Oh that's good, I thought you were stuck in this traffic behind me."

"No, because I had to go to my meeting I was forced to take a different route. Can you believe that?"

"That's great, because if you didn't have to go to that meeting and left from home you would have been stuck in this traffic and late, like me."

"I know. We have to remember this the next time there is something that seems to be getting in the way."

"That's right. Isn't it amazing? Nothing happens by mistake."

Something to remember for sure, because whenever there seems to be an unavoidable obstacle in our way, it is usually there for our own good. Some consider it God, doing for us what we could not do for ourselves. Another tool I've since found useful when inconvenience strikes and I feel like whining, "Why is this happening to me?" is to substitute it with, "Why is this happening FOR me?"

You may be thinking, yeah, well, that was a great lesson for your wife, but you were stuck in traffic for no good reason at all. Well, here's the rest of the story. The traffic did eventually open up, and even though Lori was at the party and it was no longer necessary for me to show up, I decided to do so anyway. I was so enthusiastic about how it all played out so far, why not go all the way? When I finally made it to the party, Lori's big bright smile lit up when she saw me walk in and the birthday girl's parents offered me what turned out to be the best coconut cupcake I ever ate.

HOW TO ENJOY ART LIKE A PRO: YOU EITHER LIKE IT OR YOU DON'T

Have you ever been tempted to walk into an art gallery or museum but the doorway was as far as you got? If you were afraid to step inside because you didn't want to feel stupid if you didn't understand the artwork, you are not alone. Most people are intimidated by art, including myself. But thanks to fellow artist and teacher, George A. Rada, I can now walk into any art gallery or museum and enjoy whatever art is on display, and so can you.

George and I met in 1993 at an artists' get-together held by art dealer Molly Barnes at the Roger Smith Hotel in New York City. George and I became quick friends. Over the next few years we visited each other's studios and enjoyed encouraging one another. At that time, George was a much more established artist than I, and a teacher at the prestigious Art Students League, so I would listen closely to what he had to say.

One evening he shared how his new students were often intimidated by art. He explained that the reason most people are intimidated is because they think they must understand art intellectually before they can appreciate it. Or they think they need to learn a lot more about art before ever setting foot in a gallery or museum. And trying to learn more about art can be intimidating in itself. Even art reviews tend to be more pretentious than inviting. So what's the solution? George put it simply, "The idea that you must be sophisticated or knowledgeable to appreciate fine art is erroneous." He went on to explain that the way to enjoy art like a pro is simple: you don't have to be a pro to enjoy art. Matter of fact, the less you know the better your experience.

This all may seem like B.S. since it's contrary to what you may believe, but it should come as a relief. The only thing necessary for you to do to enjoy art is to bring yourself to an art exhibit, and let the art do the work. Forget what you've read, forget all your preconceived ideas, and just allow yourself to respond to the art on display. Trust me, it works.

What will happen? You'll enjoy your own interpretation. Maybe the artwork will awaken a long forgotten memory and strong emotional feeling will wash over you. A movie may begin to play in your head starring the characters portrayed in the scene painted by the artist. There could be a strong attraction to shapes and colors that you can't quite explain yet find fascinating. You might even become inspired to create something yourself when you get home, or have the overwhelming desire to call up a friend and tell them all about the incredible time you just treated yourself to.

IF YOU'RE DEPRESSED
GET OFF YOUR ASS AND DO THE DISHES

Most kids look forward to Saturday mornings. My brother, Eric and I dreaded them. Saturday mornings we had to perform hard labor before we were allowed to play with our friends. Our father, raising us on his own, ran our house like a military boot camp. So the goal was to perform like a perfect soldier, completing assigned chores as thoroughly and quickly as possible. If they weren't done to my father's liking, I'd have to start over until they were. If he heard me complain, or sigh, he'd heap on more to do. Without a mother around to soften his blows, or pick up some of the slack, it was hell. Even the neighborhood kids learned real quick to stay clear of our house on Saturday mornings. They wouldn't even wander close to our yard for fear my father would grab them by the collar, toss them inside, and put them to work mopping the kitchen floor with Janitor in a Drum, or scrubbing the bathroom with Clorox. Since this actually happened to Todd Caldiero and Frankie Dragone, I'm pretty sure they were the ones who spread the word to avoid the Fusaro compound on Saturdays.

So it may seem absurd, because it certainly does to me, that today I am grateful for the chores I have to do. In 1986 I heard a bit of advice that, when practiced, never fails to improve my attitude: "Move a muscle, change an emotion." It may sound silly, but if you're in a funk or having a creative block, it's the best prescription there is.

This past Saturday morning is a perfect example. I felt unmotivated, and began scrolling through Facebook, which did more to depress me, than inspire. I knew exactly what to do to feel better: "Move a muscle, change an emotion." Since there were dishes in the sink, I had the perfect chore. But, as usual my thinking usually balks at any remedy that takes effort. The voice in my head chimed in, "Doing the dishes will just kill time and get in the way of the more important and worthwhile things I should be doing, like writing or cartooning."

Thanks to years of experience, I know this kind of thinking never improves my attitude, nor does it motivate me to do anything worthwhile. So with a force of will I started to wash the dishes and when they were done, I cleaned the counter top. The sense of accomplishment was so incredible I continued. It was somewhere between making the bed and cleaning the windows that I began to feel so good I was inspired to write this book. Once again, I was amazed and grateful that doing something so simple and unrelated to my problem actually resolved it.

Another miraculous by-product of this exercise is that it always seems to expand time. Not only do

I have plenty of time to perform these unrelated tasks which lift my spirits, but many other unexpected creative projects get accomplished as well (like the cartoon I drew to illustrate this story). This reinforces the belief that, as my mood lightens so does everything else. Acting on, "Move a muscle, change an emotion," has contributed to my most productive days, even if they didn't start out that way. This proves that although my day may have a rough start, with a little muscle it can end incredibly well.

> *"I got the blues thinking of the future,*
> *so I left off and made some marmalade.*
> *It's amazing how it cheers one up*
> *to shred oranges and scrub the floor."*
> - D. H. Lawrence.

Just an inch? That's everything I got!

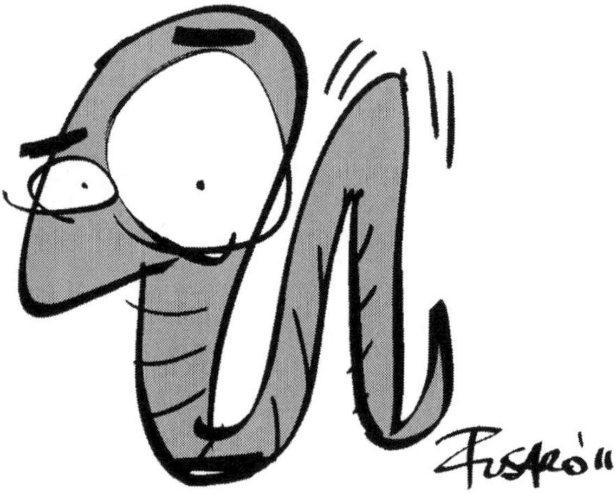

I GREW AN INCH
WHEN I QUIT ART SCHOOL
AND JOINED THE COAST GUARD

As freshmen art students we were invited to the senior art students' exhibit. I am sure the intention was to inspire the freshmen artists with a glimpse of what they too will soon be capable of. I entered the gallery with the other students, took one look around at all the incredible artwork on display and thought, "What's the use?" The enormity of ever being able to accomplish what I had seen was too much. So I left and joined the military. I figured this act of patriotism would mask my cowardice. However during my five years of active duty I did learn one of the most valuable tools for success and it came in the form of the silly little slogan, "Inch by inch, life is a cinch." Soon after my honorable discharge I decided to pick up where I had left off and re-apply to an art school.

Once I was accepted, this slogan became a regular mantra of mine. Everyday when I felt like giving up because the goal seemed too enormous for where I was at the time, I would remind myself of this simple truth, "Inch by inch, life's a cinch." It calmed me down, relieved me of self-imposed pressure and allowed me to focus on what I was doing at that moment. Rather than getting caught up in thoughts of where I thought I should be by this stage in my life and the overwhelming tasks I needed to do to get there, I began to just enjoy finishing each assignment, one by one, inch by inch.

Ironically, it did not take long for this method to start paying huge dividends. I received scholarships and awards for my work. While still a student, I was invited to become an honorary member of the NJ Art Directors Club. At the Club's reception, one of the members, who was also a college professor, asked if I would be available to speak to her students on the secret to my success. I was incredibly flattered and agreed without hesitation. When she told me where she taught I was blown away, it was the very school I had left defeated by my own outlook years before. How ironic? I left that school overwhelmed by the burden of my own doubts and now I had the opportunity to return as an inspiration. I brought hope to a new generation of art students by sharing the secret of my success: the silly little slogan, "Inch by inch, life's a cinch."

HOW I TALK MYSELF OUT OF TALKING MYSELF OUT OF WHAT I WOULD LIKE TO DO

How many projects have you talked yourself out of? It seems like every morning I'm inspired with some new creative idea to pursue but somewhere between finishing my coffee and shaving I give up without ever getting started. I can talk myself out of any worthwhile creative urge including, painting the living room a new color, drawing a new cartoon, rearranging the furniture, and even writing this book.

It's as if, as soon as I begin to feel excited about something new I would like to do, the reasons why I shouldn't start begin to surface. They're like mosquitoes–relentless. Only far deadlier to my creative well-being than mosquitoes, these doubts and excuses take a piece of enthusiasm with each bite. If I don't do something immediately, they begin to swarm and before I know it I'm overwhelmed. What's fascinating is that some of these negative thoughts some how seem quite reasonable, like they are out to protect me from harm.

I love dreaming... all the fun without the burden of deadlines.

Here are a just a few examples of what I'm talking about:

"That's a silly idea."

"It'll cost too much."

"You don't have time to do something like that."

"You're too young. No one will take you seriously."

"You're too old. No one will take you seriously."

"That's arrogant."

"What are you trying to prove?"

"Don't you have better things to do with your time? What about the lawn, the gutters; doesn't the car need an oil change?"

"You'll look ridiculous."

"It'll take too long."

"You can't do something like that by yourself and no one will want to help you. No one has time to help you."

"Why bother? No one cares."

"Don't you have enough going on? When are you going to have the time?"

"Everything is fine the way it is, why change it?"

I could go on ad nauseum.

Are these thoughts really looking out for my best interest? Not at all. It's just my fear of the unknown getting the best of me. They are just silly old beliefs born out of fear and trying to protect me from embarrassment.

The old saying, "Better the devil you know, than the devil you don't," is not always the best advice. As a matter of fact, "better safe than sorry" tends to leave me more sorry than safe when I use it to hold me back from taking a step out of my comfort zone and into the realm of creative discovery. Whenever I put off a creative nudge and justify doing so with any of the reasons I've listed, I feel dead. Like I am plodding along in a fog-colored suit merely existing. Worse, I must keep convincing myself why it makes sense not to pursue the inspired idea I had. Avoidance is a full time job.

So how do I prevent talking myself out of pursuing a creative impulse? I try to remember to treat these doubts and excuses (that come to me disguised as mature and reasonable thoughts) like unruly children clamoring for my attention. Instead of arguing with them I simply acknowledge each one as it arises and cast if off with these reassuring words: "Thank you for bringing that to my attention. Don't worry, God will help us with that." One by one they disappear. I imagine them happily skipping way into the ethers. Meanwhile, my enthusiasm remains intact and with it the momentum I need to continue on with that small but crucial first step. Soon I'm further along than expected and amazed at what I'm capable of.

"Believe your beliefs and doubt your doubts."
                    –F.F. Bosworth

MY ROTTEN MOTHER
WAS THE PERFECT MOM

"What's better than being unemployed grown men who get to hang out everyday at Starbucks 'cause we're still being supported by our mothers?"

"Telling everyone we're Screenwriters?"

I dreaded our fourth grade assembly. All the kids scampered around the classroom asking each other, "Is your mommy coming?" Without waiting for a response, they'd finish with, "MY mommy's coming!"

Over and over the same thing would bounce out of every kid's mouth but mine. I answered by nodding, "Yes" and praying to myself, "Baby Jesus, please don't let my mommy come to the assembly."

At School 9 the assemblies were held in the auditorium. It was really an indoor basketball court with a stage. Folding chairs were set up for the audience. The students from all the other grades attended and the parents of the students performing were all invited. Because the assemblies were held during the day it was usually only mommies who showed up.

Our performance began as planned. Throughout the performance I was tormented by the thought that at any moment my mother would show up while I was on stage. It wasn't until we were halfway through that I began to feel relief, "Maybe my mom's not going to make it after all." Right then a loud Ka-Chun-Ka! sound came from back of the auditorium. It was the loud sound of one of those Ka-Chun-Ka! bars. That's what we called the long brass bar handles on the doors to the auditorium. It took both hands and all your might to push one down hard enough to open a door and when you did they'd make a loud Ka-Chun-Ka! sound.

The entire audience spun around in their seats as a door flew open. Silence. Everything stopped. On stage I was frozen in shock, it felt like I was dreaming. There she was, my mommy, drunk out of her mind standing slightly off balance in the doorway. Her frosted hair was all banged up, a purse dangling off her left arm. She was wearing a tight sweater, Capri pants and heels. Oblivious to the fact that the entire audience was twisted around in their seats and staring at her in shock, she pointed at the stage and proudly shouted, "My baby!"

This prompted everyone to swing back around in their seats to see who her "baby" was. Frozen on stage, my face heated up like the coils in a toaster oven and turned just as red. With all eyes upon us I began to find comfort in the thought that maybe they'd think it's one of the other kids; after all, there are four of us standing on the stage. But as soon as she blasted out, "Daaaaa-rell!" it was over. I just wanted to fall on my cardboard sword and end it all.

Walking home from school in utter humiliation I couldn't imagine anything worse, until I heard Brazil 66's, "Mas Que Nada," blasting from the open windows of our house. When I stepped inside my mother grabbed me by my hand, pulled me into the living room and began leading me around as she danced holding a drink in her free hand.

"Come on Darrell, dance with Mommy. Maybe if you moved your ass a little more we wouldn't have to shop in the husky department."

Seeing your mother drunk is one thing, but being forced to dance with your drunken mother is a discomfort like no other. Even though no one was there to witness this, except for my younger brother, Eric (who pretended to be a cat so he wouldn't have to dance with her), the pain of humiliation was excruciating.

At five o'clock my dad walked in the back door and Mommy made a beeline for the kitchen. The crash of the silverware drawer hitting the floor was followed by my father shouting out,

"Billie, will you put down the knife!"

From past experience I knew she didn't really intend to stab my dad, she just wanted to get his attention. But this time she really wanted to teach him a lesson. While my dad tried to convince her not to kill someone with the knife, she began to strip until she was standing in the kitchen completely naked. Then she threw down the knife and ran out the back door.

"God damn it! Darrell, Eric, get out here!" my father yelled, "Your mother just ran out of the house. Naked!"

When my father caught a glimpse of me his impatience grew to outrage, "What the hell are you doing putting shoes on for? Your mother's not wearing any! Come on we're gonna lose her. We got to go get her!"

So there I was with my little brother Eric, chasing our naked mother through the neighborhood and it wasn't easy keeping up with her—she was jumping hedges like a wild gazelle. It was like and episode of *Mutual of Omaha's Wild Kingdom*. Then neighborhood porch lights began popping on like the flashing bulbs of paparazzi cameras. It wasn't until we were halfway down the block that my father was able to tackle her. Unfortunately, it was on Rhonda Manzini's front yard, a classmate of mine and the girl I had a crush on. I can still see her standing there pressed up against the screen door with her parents behind her staring at us. Now it was clear that any chance of ever winning her over was shot. From then on this girl was like kryptonite; anytime I'd see her what little self-confidence I had evaporated on the spot, nothing remained but inadequacy and the urge to hide or die.

All my friends who lived on the block were now coming outside with their parents to see what all the commotion was. They watched my dad walk my mother home as he struggled to keep her wrapped in the terry cloth robe he tackled her with. Eric and I followed, wishing we were invisible.

It wasn't long after this episode that my parents divorced and our mother moved out. I thought having her out of our lives would change how inadequate I felt. It didn't. I still felt like a turd compared to all the other kids on the School #9 playground. I knew I needed something special to transform myself from what I believed everyone thought of me, into someone they would admire.

That day came when I discovered where my dad hid his card playing money. I knew with money I could impress the other kids. So I came up with a plan. Believing my father would notice if any bills were taken, I would only take some of the change. Since my dad was at work all day, I'd walked home for lunch, steal a roll of quarters and head back to school. This was 1972 when a ten dollar roll of quarters was worth like, ten grand. So I was able to buy massive bags of Starburst fruit chews. I didn't even like Starburst fruit chews, but the cool kids did. It worked like magic. As soon as I'd arrive at the playground during our lunch recess, all the kids would crowd around me and I'd throw out Starburst fruit chews to them. It was like throwing herring to hungry sea lions. The kids went wild for these fruit chews. It was incredible, like being a Rock Star with groping fans. It worked. I was famous.

This went on for weeks. None of the adults at school questioned it. When the owner of Carousel, the local candy shop where I was buying the Starbursts, asked me where I was getting all the loot, I told him it was from allowance and shining shoes. This lie made me feel uncomfortable but not enough to stop.

While skipping home for lunch to snatch another roll of quarters I noticed my dad's car in the driveway. This was odd, he was never home at lunchtime. I panicked, "He knows!" I knew running away wasn't an option for a cowardly ten year old, so I continued toward our house trying to come up with a plausible lie. Before I got up the front steps the screen door swung open, my dad was looking down at me, "Darrell I want to talk to you. Someone's been taking rolls of quarters from my card money."

Bracing myself as he continued. "Have you seen your mother around here, lately?"

I stood in shock and slowly nodded, "Yes."

Only ten years old and I threw my mother under the bus.

The years following this incident flew by without our mother around. Her leaving us became my great excuse for all sorts of irresponsibility and bad behavior, especially when I got caught. When I was eighteen our father died and I was lost. Failing miserably at life, I was full of self-pity and quick to blame all my problems on our mother leaving us.

At twenty-four years old, unable to lower my standards as fast as my behavior, I hit bottom. It took a military Court Martial for me to realize that my problems were of my own making, no one else was to blame. I'll be forever grateful to the U.S. Marine Corps Gunnery Sergeant who made it painfully clear that the only options I had left were to either change or die.

It was during this time, motivated to change, that I reached out to renew a relationship with my mother. It had been many years since I had been in touch with her. When I contacted her she was very happy to hear from me, but because she left when I was so young, the best way to describe how I felt would be, ambivalent. Over the years I continued to keep in touch with her via letters, postcards, and phone calls telling her I loved her. Still I was doing this mostly because I felt I ought to.

Then about fifteen years later, out of nowhere, guilt over stealing those darn quarters began to resurface. Should I say something to my mother and admit what I did and apologize?

Feeling like I should apologize and justifying why I shouldn't went back and forth in my head. When the urge to apologize came up I'd stuff it down with reasons why it wasn't necessary. Telling myself that it wasn't a big deal. I was only a kid. It happened so long ago, besides, she left us. She's lucky I'm talking to her at all.

From then on every time I thought of my mother I'd remember the quarters and have to wrestle with why I should or should not apologize. It was becoming clear to me that my continuing to justify not apologizing was the indicator that I should. So I threw in the towel, asked God for courage and called her. The conversation went like this:

"Mom, remember when I was little and you got blamed for stealing the quarters from daddy's card playing money? I lied to Daddy. I was stealing them and blamed you. I feel really bad about doing that. I'm sorry."

She responded kindly, "Isn't it funny the silly things we do when we are young?" and then after a long pause, her voice quivered, "Darrell, I don't want to go to my grave with you and Eric thinking that I didn't love you both." She began to cry, "The hardest thing I ever did was to leave you boys, and it kills me to think how much I loved you both and that you both probably think I didn't."

A warm feeling grew in my chest. Wonderful moments began to bubble up to the surface of my heart. Memories of my mom teaching me how to tie my shoes, how she'd never get frustrated and praised me continuously for the slightest improvement. I remembered her teaching me how to color in the lines of the coloring book and her sharing her secret on how to make the images pop by applying more pressure to the crayon along the outline of the drawing. All of a sudden I was struck hard by the clear recollection that while I was a small boy she always told me how special I was and that I would do amazing things when I grew up. I felt compelled to let her know that I remembered how wonderful she was; it came out simply, "We know you loved us. I love you, Mommy."

Funny how this all came about by admitting my faults, rather than demanding that she acknowledge hers. Now when I look back, my mother's behavior doesn't seem that rotten at all. Did my mother intend to humiliate me by pointing me out at the school assembly or wanting me to dance with her that day? Not at all. I believe she drank because it freed her from the overwhelming insecurity she had about raising us, and that she only wished to include me with her in the brief moments of release that alcohol allowed her to enjoy. In any case, it is obvious now that if it wasn't for my mother being exactly the way she was, my life would not have turned out as well as it has. Looks like my rotten mother was the perfect mom all along.

JUST GIVE UP AND SAY THANK YOU

Ed Biagiotti, my co-host on our talk radio show *Funniest Thing! with Darrell and Ed*, was having trouble getting started one morning. His son didn't want to go to school. Ed felt himself getting frustrated but rather than attempting to intimidate and coerce his son into compliance, he decided to bless the situation instead. So Ed stepped outside onto his porch, took a deep breath and simply said, "Thank you." This simple act relieved him of the burden of forcing his will and things miraculously fell into place. Ed and his son were soon happily on their way to school.

"If the only prayer you said was thank you, that would be enough." – Meister Eckhart

THE 3 QUESTIONS
THAT KEEP ME OUT OF HOT WATER

1. Does it NEED to be said?
2. Does it NEED to be said RIGHT NOW?
3. Does it NEED to be said BY ME?

THE KEY TO GREAT STORYTELLING

THANKS TO ALPHONSO D'ABRUZZO, A.K.A. ALAN ALDA

I recently came across this simple and easy-to-remember key to telling a great story. Like most valuable things in life, I stumbled upon it seemingly by coincidence. It happened when I decided to grab a cup of coffee from a local coffee shop other than Starbucks. At the time this was a huge step out of my comfort zone. But, I had no choice since our local Starbucks was closed that week for renovations. So, on this particular day and under these circumstances, the Rumor Mill Cafe turned out to be the most convenient place for friend and co-host Ed Biagiotti and I to meet for our regular afternoon coffee. I ordered a large drip and since Ed hadn't arrived yet, I decided I'd flip through one of the donated books these non-franchise independently owned coffee shops tend to have laying around for customers to read. On top of the short pile of books was Alan Alda's autobiography, *Never Have Your Dog Stuffed: And Other Things I've Learned.*

Although I'm not a huge Alan Alda fan, I do know he lives in New Jersey and his real name is Alphonso D'Abruzzo. Since he and I had the Italian New Jersey connection I figured, what the hell, and decided to check it out. So I picked up his book and sat down at a two-top table. I opened up the book to the very first page with the following quote:

"Act One: Get your hero up a tree.
Act Two: Throw rocks at him.
Act Three: Get him down out of the tree.
- attributed to George Abbott, on playwriting"

This is the best description of effective storytelling I've ever read. Whether it's in the form of a play, screenplay, cartoon strip, or book, it applies. The best advice is always true, simply stated, and easy to remember. I've since shared Mr. Abbott's quote with students as part of my collegiate presentations. They appreciate it. It clicks with them too.

So for this one, thank you Starbucks for being closed, thank you Rumor Mill Cafe for being the only convenient option available that day, thank you Ed Biagiotti for showing up late, thank you whoever you are for donating Alan Alda's autobiography to the Rumor Mill, thank you George Abbott for putting this great advice so bluntly, and thank you Alan Alda for feeling so strongly about George Abbott's advice you decided to quote him on the very first page of your book where I would find it.

"Nothing, absolutely nothing happens in God's world by mistake." - Alcoholics Anonymous

GET THE BEST OF BOTH WORLDS
(HERE AND THE HEREAFTER)
ALL FOR JUST $5,000!

Last week I met my friend Mike Dugan in downtown Los Angeles to see his new place. It only cost him $5,000 and it is literally to die for. He calls it his downtown condo and it's located on the corner of Temple Street & Grande Avenue, directly across from the Frank Gehry designed Walt Disney Concert Hall.

Who said there are no more real estate bargains in Los Angeles? They exist, but only for those who can really accept the unavoidable reality that one day this life will come to an end. Why is that? Because these "downtown condos" are located in the mausoleum at the Cathedral of Our Lady of Angels. It's true, just like my friend Mike, you too can be entombed in the cellar of the Cathedral for as little as $5,000.

I appreciate Mike's new "condo" because ironically it relieves my fear of death. This is good news because as long as I can remember I've dreaded death. As an eight year old, I was overly concerned about being drafted to and dying in the Vietnam War when I turned eighteen. The prayer, "Now I lay me down to sleep, I pray the Lord my soul to keep, but if I die before I wake, I pray the

Lord my soul to take," that my grandmother made me recite with her as she tucked me in at night was terrifying. I didn't want to die in my sleep. At the time being too embarrassed to let anyone know about my fear, I kept it to myself. Big mistake. I am sure if I had confided in someone I would have been relieved to discover I wasn't the only one who was afraid of death.

Death may be inevitable but the fear of it doesn't have to be constantly lingering in the shadows. My friend Mike is a living example of how the acceptance of death adds joy to living. Thanks to him I have been able to find peace of mind by changing my perception of death. I've come to see it as a part of life, and not the end of it. I also encourage myself with that fact that it can't be that bad if it's the one thing, other than being born, that we all have in common. However, I still get a little creeped out by the paperwork for a simple procedure at the hospital when it refers to power of attorney and how to divvy up my organs in case of death. So in these rare instances I find just diving right in with faith and signing without too much thought (or reading) frees my spirit of unnecessary worry. Accepting this fact of death, rather than fearing it, trying to avoid thinking about it, or denying it, helps me appreciate every moment and everybody in my life more fully. In this healthy frame of mind strangers become fellow travelers and allowing someone ahead of me in traffic is a pleasure instead of an irritating obligation. Funny how the acceptance of death has the unlikely effect of adding life to your life.

WHAT LITTLE BROTHERS ARE FOR

"Here, you go first!" That may be the thing my little brother remembers me telling him most.

I'm not sure how this tiny little drawing got in my pocket-sized pad but, for better or worse, it speaks volumes about my relationship with my little brother. When we were young I was the schemer, always coming up with incredible plans for us to implement. He was always the reluctant partici- pant, who had to be coaxed by my carnival barker enthusiasm as to why this time everything would go as planned, and I promised we weren't going to get in trouble. Rarely did it go as planned and we always got in trouble.

The amazing thing is that no matter how many times my schemes failed, and no matter how many times my brother suffered the consequences of my bright ideas, he always supported me. I'm old enough now to admit that I would have been a very lonely little boy, afraid to try anything by myself if it weren't for my little brother, who was always willing to support me despite the known risks. He believed in me because he loved me, no matter how crazy my ideas may have been.

Today his belief in me lives somewhere deep inside of me and encourages me whenever I step into a new adventure.

Why have I spent all this time at home drawing Cartoons and not out sketching hot babes?

I WAS DISCOVERED ON A BOAT IN THE BERING SEA

We all have talent, something we enjoy doing so much that it rarely if ever feels like work. As a boy, I would often fantasize about how wonderful it would be to earn a living drawing cartoons. I'd imagine myself living like cartoonist Charles Schultz as I'd seen in pictures of him at his drawing table, cheerfully illustrating the daily adventures of his *Peanuts*. For me that seemed like the ultimate dream job. However, my life seemed to take quite a different course. In 1984 I enlisted in the U.S. Coast Guard. Shortly after boot camp, we drew straws to see who would end up having to do a tour aboard the U.S. Coast Guard Cutter *Jarvis*. This was one of the Coast Guard's long range ships, which meant prolonged time underway at sea.

Ever hear the saying, "Do what you love and the money will follow"? Well, it was obvious that wasn't going to be happening to me anytime soon. I drew the shortest straw. The *Jarvis* was scheduled to patrol the Bering Sea. I wasn't happy. My fantasy about life in the U.S. Coast Guard was to be sun-tanned aboard a flashy speedboat like I had seen on the TV show *Miami Vice*. My reality however was about to be more like the TV series, *Deadliest Catch*. I'll never forget that moment of pulling away from the dock in Honolulu about to set sail to

Alaskan waters berating myself, "Now look what you got yourself into!"

Once out at sea, my days consisted entirely of mindless grunt work. Being the lowest ranking sailor on board I mainly chipped paint and then repainted the areas I just chipped, cleaned and organized areas that were in desperate need of organizing and cleaning, and I was also assigned trash detail. The only time I got a break from these chores was when I had to stand watch outside in the frigid cold, above the bridge in the crow's nest I scanned the horizon for anything out of the ordinary. When my duties were finished I would draw. Thinking ahead, I had packed plenty of paper, pencils and markers for this tour of duty.

This was good old days before smart phones and satellite TV. So that meant the only form of shipboard entertainment was either playing cards with other sailors, reading a book, or smoking cigarettes on the fantail. Instead, I spent each night drawing cartoons based on my daily experience at sea. It became the highlight of my day. Soon, I began to see each day's mishap as content for my next cartoon. Crazy as this may seem, a day without some sort of challenge or comical blunder on my part was seen as a disappointment. When I showed my cartoons to two shipmates they were impressed.

"You should show these to the captain!" one of them suggested.

"Really?"

"Yeah, he'd love them!" said the other.

I did and they were right. The captain loved them so much he immediately assigned me the task of creating a new cartoon every day to tack up on "the board" in the main pass each morning. The board was the only bulletin board on the ship. This was where the entire crew was expected to look to for each day's itinerary as laid out in the P.O.D., Plan Of the Day, written and posted by the ship's executive officer. It was located in the main pass directly outside the galley where it couldn't be missed. It was encased in plexiglass under lock and key. Only the executive officer had a key and was granted permission to hang the approved notices therein. Although flattered, I was apprehensive. Sharing my drawings with a few close friends is one thing, but the entire crew? Plus, this meant it was no longer a pastime for me. In addition to my regular daily duty assignments I was now under orders to create new cartoon every evening.

The captain displayed his confidence by trusting me with a key to the bulletin board case. He then surprised me with access to very my own designated art studio on the ship. There was an available drawing table located in the ship's Marine Safety Office and from then on it was all mine. That meant no more fighting to find an open table somewhere to draw, nor did I have to unpack and repack my pens and pencils every evening. So I began. Each evening after duty I'd complete a new cartoon and in the morning hang it in the main pass alongside the Plan Of the Day.

Some nights I found it hard to sleep because I was so excited to share what I drew with the crew in the morning. I became a bit of a celebrity too. Sailors would make it a point to pull me aside and tell me how much they enjoyed a specific cartoon. Pretty soon, putting up the morning cartoon became a major event. The sailors would crowd around the bulletin board after breakfast and wait patiently as I pushed my way through the crowd to unlock the case and post my latest one.

Looking forward to drawing at each day's end made tending to my regular duties seem effortless. I was happy, but there was a conspiracy brewing. I was called in to see the captain. He told me that a couple of the chief petty officers were wondering if I could be given a new daily duty assignment and the he agreed with them. From that moment on I was relieved of all my previous daily grunt work. My new full-time shipboard job was to create and paint murals on designated doors of the ship—all to be done in my unique style of cartooning. If this hadn't happened to me personally I would have never believed it possible.

On the last day of our tour, the Plan Of the Day item number three read: "Also, a good job to Darrell 'The Door Painter' Fusaro, for his artwork on the doors to sick bay, supply office, hobby shop, ship's office, and the barber pole. I'm glad the Coast Guard doesn't pay by the hour but he has done a lot to improve many of the spaces aboard *JARVIS*." It was official, under the most absurd of circumstances my dream became a reality —I was a professional cartoonist.

"I am hemmed in by what seems like a very real doubt of myself. But if I use my own true talents, the way will open out before me. I need not work to make this true. IT IS TRUE." -Emmet Fox

HOW YOU PRESENT IT
IS HOW THEY'LL PERCEIVE IT

If you are wondering what breed of dog I have, she's an Australian brindle hound. Her disposition is as pleasant and loving as the name sounds. I have to confess, she wasn't always an Australian brindle hound. She used to be a pit bull. Can you believe it?

It was horrible. In the past, every time Lori and I would be out with Gabby, we would dread it when people would inquire as to what breed of dog she was. As soon as we answered, "She's a pit bull," the color would drain from their faces and if they happened to have a child with them they'd snatch them up quickly with an accusing look that registered, "How could you?"

We would catch ourselves beginning to over compensate, explaining how sweet she is, that we have two cats she loves, that not all pit bulls are bad, that it depends how they are raised, etc. . . . It was so much work. I would even fire off a quick pit bull history lesson on how at the turn of last century, the pit bull, a.k.a. American Staffordshire terrier, was considered America's sweetheart breed. Theodore Roosevelt had one. The Buster Brown dog was a pit bull, and so was Petey from the *Little Rascals*. The Wells Fargo Bank mascot was a pit, and even Helen Keller's guide dog was a pit bull. All fascinating stuff, but it never seemed to convince anyone. Besides it was exhausting.

Then, something wonderful happened. One day while Lori and I were having lunch at an outdoor cafe with Gabby, a couple at the next table asked the dreaded question. "What kind of dog is that?" I took a deep breath and tentatively let it out, "She's a pit bull." "I thought so." the lady said, "We had a pit bull exactly like her. She was so sweet. She loved our grandkids." Lori and I were overjoyed. I began to tell the woman how most people freak out when they hear she is a pit bull. While the lady was loving up Gabby she said, "I know isn't that terrible? My husband would tell people that ours was an Australian brindle hound." Lori and I were blown away. Could it be that simple?

From that day on Gabby was no longer a pit bull. She was now an Australian brindle hound. It was miraculous. Everyone loves an Australian brindle hound. Some people even told us how they could tell that Gabby was an Australian brindle hound by her sweet disposition. At first I was concerned about being deceptive, but realized introducing Gabby as an Australian brindle hound wasn't deceptive, introducing her as a pit bull was. Although Australian brindle hounds only exist in that wonderfully sweet and loving part of everyone's imagination, so does the ferocious pit bull. So just like someone once said, "I thought she was an Australian brindle hound by her sweet disposition," she must be.

THE BEST WAY TO MAKE A BAD IMPRESSION
IS BY TRYING TO MAKE A GOOD ONE

When I was 17, my father was in the hospital. He had been raising my younger brother and myself on his own, since I was 8 and my brother 4. Now, he was really sick with colon cancer, and although he was only 39 years old, he looked like a frail old man.

I was always intimidated by my father and could never seem to do anything he would have considered admirable. Trying one more time to prove to him that I was respectable and protect me from his berating me, I decided to invite John, a neighborhood friend of mine, to join me to visit with my father at the hospital. John went to a Catholic high school, had great parents, was a straight arrow and my father respected him. So it seemed like a great idea. It seemed so good that in addition to John, I also thought it would really impress my father to meet my new girlfriend, Holly. She was tall, smart, beautiful, tan and blonde. I was convinced that by bringing them along with me my father would be impressed and say so.

On the way to the hospital, I was enthusiastic, gabbing a mile a minute with John and Holly. At the hospital, I walked into my Dad's room, followed by

Holly and then John. I was beaming, confident that my father would be impressed by the company I keep. He looked us over and then turned to John and said, "What the fuck are you doing with this loser? He's like having a fucking anchor around your neck. Do yourself a favor and cut him loose before he drags you down with him."

Right after that, my father told me to get out of the room because he said looking at me made him sick. John spent a few minutes more in the room with my Dad and then we left. John was as kind as he could be, not saying anything on the ride home and I didn't utter a peep as I drove. We drove in silence, I couldn't wait to drop them off. I never called Holly again.

That was one of the last times I saw my father in the hospital before he died. Years have gone by and I have realized what a serious blunder I made. I never for once considered that my father might have been embarrassed about the physical condition he was in, and that having unexpected guests let alone strangers sprung on him like that was that last thing he would want, or expect from his eldest son. Instead of trying to impress my father by bringing an entourage with me to the hospital, I believe he would have been more impressed if I had showed up by myself and spent some time with him alone.

Today John is still a straight arrow and has grown into the successful family man my father would have expected. Not to long ago I ran into Holly's brother at a school reunion and he pulled me aside to tell me something he felt was important to say to me. It was that Holly once told him that out of all the guys she knew, I was one she always thought highly of. I guess she saw in me what my father did and I couldn't, that he loved me for who I was, not who I was trying so hard to pretend to be.

DON'T LET REASON SLIP YOU A ROOFIE

I just finished a delicious egg white, spinach & feta wrap at a local coffee shop when the idea for a new cartoon flashed in my mind. I had my pen but I didn't have my drawing paper. What should I do? I didn't want to let this one get away. I could sketch it out on the paper bag my wrap came in. That's the moment reason tried to slip me a roofie with the following thoughts, "You can't draw on that bag. It'll look like crap!"

"Yeah, and what if by chance the drawing turns out so well on the bag that you can't replicate it on good paper later? That'll really be a bummer."

"Relax and enjoy your coffee. You can draw it later at home, on the proper paper."

As I tried to shrug these reasonable excuses off, they grew deadlier, "Are you sure this idea for a cartoon is even a good one?"

Which quickly morphed into, "That idea is stupid."

And the final blow struck below the belt, "Why bother? What the hell are you so excited about drawing this cartoon for anyway? Just to show your friends on Facebook? Boy, is that lame."

Miraculously, I ignored these thoughts, smoothed out my wrinkled wrap bag and got started. Happily, like every other time I acted on inspiration rather than doing what seemed reasonable, I was thrilled with the results. The cartoon seemed to magically draw itself. There was no need to redraw it on 'proper' paper when I got home either. It was perfect—created the moment inspiration struck on a used paper sandwich bag while sitting in a coffee shop. See for yourself, it's the cartoon on page 34 of this book.

"To live intuitively is to live fourth-dimensionally."
– Claude Bragdon

"Dude, I had no idea you were that angry."

BLESS YOUR MISERABLE BOSS AND SHE'LL LOVE YOU FOR IT

In 2003, I was running a small Public Access TV studio in Marina del Rey, CA when I was told by my manager that I was going to be assigned another TV production facility in Los Angeles to supervise. The additional studio was where our network CNN news program was produced which meant a step up for me. However, he warned me about what I already knew, this place had been a hornet's nest for years and it was probably going to be extremely difficult before it got easy. There was an existing manager there who for some reason didn't like me. This became very apparent when one of my newly assigned crew members confided in me that I better watch my back. He went on to explain that she told everyone in the studio that, and I quote, "If Darrell Fusaro so much as peeps anything that can possibly be misconstrued as harassment I'm going to make sure he goes down."

My feelings ran the gamut from worry, panic, hurt, anger, self-pity, and finally, surrender. I knew deep down that no amount of self-will could manipulate the situation in my favor. So I put all my faith in the power of love and adopted the simple truth, "Bless a thing and it will bless you. Curse it and it will curse you." as my guide. In spite of dreading having to interact with her each day, I applied the following. When thoughts of fear, worry and/or anger came up, I would sweep them aside by blessing the situation. I'd do this by choosing to think thoughts of love, happiness and success for her. I'd pray for her to receive every good thing that I'd want for myself. Some days, this came easy—others, not so much. For instance, one time I pulled into the lot and noticed that her car was parked in the handicapped space. It took every ounce of willpower to not call the authorities to have her car ticketed and towed. Instead, I blessed her and let it go.

In less than a month, with no coercion on my part, things began to improve. She initiated pleasant conversations. Visitors to the studio would comment how pleasant it felt to be there. Since she was a long time Los Angeles resident, she would recommend hip local weekend outings for Lori and I. One of my crazy habits at the studio was to break into short songs at unexpected moments, something she detested—but not anymore. Now she'd pick up where I left off, by singing the next verse as loudly as I. I actually looked forward to seeing her each day. Things had improved so much that those who knew her often joked that I was putting something in her coffee. We continued to enjoy each other's company at that studio until we moved on in our separate careers.

"Life is a reflex of mental states." - Emmet Fox

IF YOU'RE INVITED TO A BIKER PARTY
GO!

In 1992 I was living in Little Falls, N.J. and attending art school. During the summer, I would often set up my easel outside my place and paint. One of my neighbors was a biker named Frank. He enjoyed watching me paint and would come over to talk whenever he saw me outside. The first week of August, we crossed paths and he invited me to a party he was throwing that weekend. I was happy to be invited, but all his friends were bikers and I really didn't know any of them so I declined. Besides, I didn't have any tattoos and these were real bikers, not 40-year-old accountants who suffering a mid-life crisis bought leather chaps, a Harley and pretended they were tough guys. So I didn't think I'd fit in. Oh, and I almost forgot, I already had plans to meet up with a girl for a date that same day, so I thanked Frank for the invitation and let him know I wouldn't be able to attend.

"Well if you change your mind, come on by. You are always welcome." Frank said as he walked away.

The weekend came, and the girl I had a date with was missing in action. I couldn't get in touch with her. So rather than pout, I took my easel outside and started on a new painting.

While I was painting two beautiful girls—a blonde and a brunette—were walking down the sidewalk. They seemed to be lost. I had a hunch they were probably looking for Frank's party.

"Are you looking for the party?" I yelled out.

"Yes!" They said.

So I pointed them towards Frank's place. As they walked off, I returned to painting. After a moment I thought, "The heck with this." I packed up my easel, threw everything into my apartment and headed to Frank's party. His place was loud and packed wall-to-wall with bikers and their girlfriends. Everyone was dressed in black and mostly leather. They were covered with tattoos, had various piercings and were all drinking beers. I spotted the blonde from outside at the food table. She was talking with a bald-headed biker who had what looked to be a tattoo of a bullet going into side of his head. Then when he turned around I saw that he had a tattoo of his brains blasting out of the other side of his head. With that I decided the blonde he was talking to was off limits.

So, I did the only thing I knew to do in situations where I don't know many people and feel uncomfortable —be of service. I asked Frank if he needed any help. He did, with something to do, I began to feel like part of the party. I picked up empty bottles and empty plates. I got his guests fresh beers from the ice chest. Gave directions to where the bathroom was and emptied ashtrays. All this made me feel very comfortable mingling among the bikers and their girlfriends. I was beginning to have a good time—except when I would catch a glimpse of myself in the big mirror Frank had hanging in the living room.

I made a bad judgment call a few days before the party and got one of those long on top, one length Michael Hutchence (the lead singer of INXS) haircuts. But mine came out more like Moe from the *Three Stooges*. Most of the time, I was able to remain in denial by avoiding looking at myself. That ended when one of Frank's friends, "Joker," who met me sometime before the haircut shouted out from across the room, "What the hell happened to you? Why did you cut your hair like that man? It used to look good!"

Anyway, I was standing by the bar to see if the old guy Frank hired to make mixed drinks needed anything when the brunette, the one who I first saw outside lost with the blonde, made her way over and sparked up a conversation about art with me. Her name was Stella and she explained that Frank's girlfriend was her beautician and had told her that I was a 'famous' artist. I wasn't famous, but I wasn't about to call Frank's girlfriend a liar. Besides I was enjoying the attention.

Stella jumped right in by asking me if I ever go to The Met. I knew she meant the Metropolitan Museum of Art in New York City. Of course I'd been to the Met.

"Yes," I said.

With that she immediately began rambling on about how her favorite gallery at The Met was the Egyptian, something or other. Right then and there I knew I was out of my league. She continued by rattling off historical dates, time periods, dynasties, and an abridged history of Egyptian art. I had no idea what the hell she was talking about—but I looked interested.

When she was all done, she asked, "So, what's your favorite gallery at the Met?"

At that moment I quickly sized things up, she's smart and great looking. Which meant I better pretend I know what she is talking about and say I like some important gallery at The Met as well. Should I tell her I liked the modern art gallery? What if it's not called that? Maybe I should just pretend to love whatever she said; I'll just repeat the stuff she said back to her. But I really wasn't paying close enough attention and could never repeat any of those hard-to-pronounce words she was saying.

So I just blurted out the truth: "My favorite room at the Met is the bookstore!"

She was silent and looked at me like she didn't hear me correctly. I knew it didn't sound impressive but, and this was surprising even to me, I didn't care. It felt good, because it was true. I love the

bookstore! I love looking at all the books, souve-
nirs, interesting toys and gadgets. It felt so great
to just tell the truth that I continued to describe
everything I enjoyed at The Met bookstore. During
my enthusiastic ranting, her friend, the blonde she
came to the party with, had made her way over to
join us and was listening in.

"Are you talking about the bookstore at The Met?"
the blonde asked.

"Yeah!" I exclaimed.

"My uncle manages that bookstore," she said.

We hit it off, talking about what a coincidence that
was, then more about the bookstore and her uncle.
She told me how she lived in New York City and
her friend, Stella, dragged her to the party because
Stella didn't want to go alone. But, the most significant thing she told me was, the guy with the bullet
tattoo on his head was just someone who struck up
a conversation with her at the food table, and not
her boyfriend.

The blonde, whose name is Lori, and I have been
together everyday since—over twenty years. Even
we're amazed it's been over twenty years. I've
been in relationships for less than twenty days
that have felt like over twenty years. It amazes
me to think how a little lie to get what I thought
was good for me would have ruined my chance of
getting what turned out to be best for me.

*"A lie may take care of the present,
but it has no future."* - Author Unknown

DO IT YOURSELF "AS SEEN ON TV"

One Saturday morning when I was about eleven years old a couple of neighborhood kids, John Zelenka and Eddie Rizzuto, rolled into our cul de sac with a brand new go-cart. It was magnificent. The kind that you race down a hill in. John sat inside and, after Eddie gave him a push, he drove down the hill. It was like he was driving a real car. It even had a steering wheel! I asked them where they got it and they said that their fathers' bought it from Sears and built it for them. They also made it clear that it was theirs and no one else could ride in it.

I ran inside and saw my dad seated at the dining room table. All I could see of him were his hands, one with a lit cigar between his fingers, and both holding up the newspaper in front of his face. I asked him, "Dad, did you see the go-cart Mr. Zelenka and Mr. Rizzuto made for John and Eddie? They got it from Sears."

"That's nice," my father said from behind the paper. "That's nice," meant, "Don't bother asking for one."

I walked back outside I had a flash of inspiration. We could make our own go-cart. It would be easy. The Little Rascals did it!

I watched *The Little Rascals* every morning before school. They were my inspiration. Here were a bunch of misfit kids who seemed to be on their own like us. Us being my younger brother Eric, our cousin Little Tommy, neighborhood friend Charlie Wapner, and me. I really believed that if the Little Rascals did it, we could too.

It was the episode titled, *Hey Neighbor!* that made building our own go-cart seem so easy to me. In this episode, a rich kid moves into the neighborhood with a brand new fire engine go-cart. He snubs the Little Rascals and rides off with the neighborhood sweetheart. Determined to win her back, the Little Rascals set out to build their own go-cart with whatever odds and ends they can scavenge from the neighborhood. In the end, through a series of mishaps and dumb luck, they win a race and get the girl.

We'll show John and Eddie, and their dads. We'll build our own go-cart. So we began by doing exactly what the Little Rascals did. Simple. Like following a recipe. Charlie and I scoured dumpsters behind the manufacturing plants in our town. We carried home all the junk that we thought could be useful, including a big metal pulley gear that would be our steering wheel.

We found everything we needed: wood, metal, screws, hinges, brackets, nuts, bolts, and on the side of Route 3, the highway that ran behind our house, a discarded gallon can of bright orange road sign paint. We dragged it all back into our garage and built our go-cart. Our wheels, from a discarded baby carriage were just like in the episode of *The Little Rascals*. They worked great in the show, but unfortunately not for us. They were way too slow. We couldn't even roll down hill. It looked as if it was all for nothing. I should have known.

Disappointed about our wheels, I sat on our back porch and told the whole story to Joey Latoracco's feet, while he worked under his car. Joey Latoracco was overweight, a lot older than us and was always working on his car in his parent's driveway. When I finished, he said, "I got a set of wheels. Real Soap Box Derby wheels from when I was your age."

He squeezed out from under his car, "You want to check them out?"

I had no idea what a Soap Box Derby was but it sounded impressive. I followed Joey up into his attic and there they were, a set of bright red metal wheels with thin black rubber treads and steel rod axles. Then he spun a wheel and made a point to demonstrate how it will continue to spin indefinitely. I was hypnotized thinking of how we must have these wheels. Then he said, "You can have them for five dollars." Five dollars? Where the hell was I going to get five dollars? This was 1973 and I was only 11 years old. Five dollars was a fortune. I had no other choice, I had to ask my father for the five dollars.

"Five dollars for a set of wheels for a go-cart?" my father answered.

I nodded.

"Tell him you'll give him $2.50."

Why couldn't my dad just give me the five dollars? We were sunk without those wheels. Joey was back under his car when I offered $2.50, and his muffled response from underneath the car was firm, "Five dollars or forget about it."

There had to be another way to get the five dollars we needed. Then it hit me. Charlie's father, Mr. Wapner. I got a hold of Charlie and brought him to Joey Latoracco's, hoping the demonstration would help convince him to ask his father for the five dollars. It did, and Mr. Wapner agreed to come with us to the Latoracco's. Mr. Wapner looked over the wheels and then wanted to talk with me and Charlie outside. He was very serious and explained that he would pay for the wheels under the condition that we . . . I still can't remember what the condition was but whatever it was, we agreed to it! Mr. Wapner paid for the wheels and Charlie and I carried them right into my garage.

We attached the wheels the chassis with U-bolts, rolled up the garage door, and then Charlie, Little Tommy and Eric pushed me out in our very own go-cart. Just like in the episode of *The Little Rascals*, it was time for our showdown with John and Eddie and their store-bought-father-assembled go-cart. The race to the bottom of the hill.

Our cul de sac was at the top of a slight hill, about twenty yards before the cross street, Woodridge Road. The entire length of our street, Sussex Road, was about a quarter of a mile long before the traffic signal at the busy intersection of Allwood Road and Market Street.

As I sat in the driver's seat, I was pushed up to the top of the cul de sac by Charlie and Little Tommy. Soon I was positioned along side our opponents. John was in the driver's seat of their go-cart and Eddie was standing in the street right behind him. Our go-cart looked huge next to theirs. The body, made of discarded plywood painted bright orange looked more like a coffin than it did a go-cart. It came to a point in the front and it had a ledge on the back. We added the ledge so whoever gave the starting push could jump on and ride along too.

Charlie joined Eric at the bottom of the hill, where the cross street, Woodridge Road, was the finish line. They were there to signal us to start the race when the coast was clear of any on-coming cars. Eddie stood behind Johnny to give him the initial push off, and Little Tommy was behind me to do the same. We settled on Little Tommy to be the pusher, because he never feared getting injured doing something absurd. This was important because we weren't sure if the ledge on the back would be safe when he jumped aboard.

Then came the signal from Eric and Charlie, the coast was clear. Little Tommy pushed and jumped aboard. Eddie gave Johnny a good shove and let him go. We rolled down the hill, passing Johnny and then past Eric and Charlie. We crossed the finish line first! And we kept on going.

"John's slowing down and stopping." Little Tommy was giving me the blow by blow of what was going on behind us as he hung on the back. We were amazed we won and were quickly approaching the Manzini's house, the half-way marker to the traffic light. Because of the grade of the street, we were still picking up speed. We could see the traffic light ahead. It was red. Johnny and the rest of the gang seemed miles behind us now. It felt like what Joey Latoracco said was true, that the wheels would continue to spin indefinitely. We had a braking system, a wooden board that would drag against the ground when pulled up hard, just like I saw on the Little Rascals' go-cart. But, just like theirs, it wasn't slowing us down and we were quickly approaching the light. In a panic, Little Tommy attempted to slow us down by dragging his feet, but the weight of the cart and our momentum was making it impossible to stop. Then we both heard the loud mechanical click from the big steel box on the corner. From years of crossing that intersection, we knew what that meant, the light was about to change. Little Tommy lifted up his feet as the light turned green and we sped right on through the major downtown intersection. Traffic was stopped at every corner. Pedestrians froze in place and watched as Little Tommy and I drove straight on through traffic like a real automobile.

We crossed Allwood Road and Market Street. As we cruised through the intersection, I turned the steering wheel, we made from a pulley, and veered left down the street between the Buster Brown Shoe Store and the corner liquor store. We coasted for another fifty yards as the street leveled off and then we slowed to a stop.

Eric and Charlie showed up on their bikes. They were as amazed as we were, asking us, "What happened? What was it like? We saw you keep going and when we lost sight of you we were worried what would happen at the light."

Little Tommy and I pushed the cart back toward our house repeating the entire story back to them in every detail as they walked their bikes along-side us. We did it just like the Little Rascals did. My childlike belief that if the Little Rascals could do it, we could too, was enough to activate The Universe to conspire in our favor.

Ironically, today I live just a few blocks from where *The Little Rascals* series was filmed in Culver City, CA. I had no idea when we purchased our home that my neighborhood was that of my childhood heroes. I discovered this fact while on jog. At the corner of National Boulevard and Washington Boulevard, underneath a large shade tree there is a bronze marker indicating the spot where Hal Roach Studios once stood. It's inscribed, 'Site of The Hal Roach Studios, Laugh Factory To The World, 1919 - 1963.' Home of *The Little Rascals*.

END ROAD RAGE WITH BIG BOY SYSTEM FOR SUCCESS

Some people have plastic saints mounted on their dashboards as protection against driving hazards. I've found having a Bob's Big Boy on the dash much more effective. At first, I thought mounting a plastic Bob's Big Boy on my dash would make me look cool, instead it's increased my humility and I'm grateful that it has. Turning out to be more corny than cool, with a Bob's Big Boy on my dash I find I'm less apt to act out when frustrated in traffic. Imagining myself red faced and bug eyed, giving another driver the finger as I speed pass them with my balding head and a Bob's Big Boy on the dash is embarrassing.

Catching a glimpse of Bob's Big Boy grinning at me while holding a hamburger up in his left hand coerces me to be more tolerant, patient and considerate than I would be otherwise. "I wouldn't do that if I were you," his little grin implies. Although this was forced humility at first, I've come to be motivated by the benefits. It seems I get to wherever I am going with less stress, more joy, and most important, no regrets. Which I am always grateful for. Especially, when I discover the other driver I was about to stick it to is actually tougher than I. I can usually tell that by the bandanna, tank top and tattoos I notice they're wearing as I pass them.

"Nothing pays off like restraint of pen and tongue." - Bill Wilson

THE BIG WINNERS
WALK AWAY EMPTY-HANDED

Growing up in New Jersey, Memorial Day was a big deal. As kids we all knew what the holiday signified; the first weekend at the shore! It was well worth listening to my father gripe about the traffic we sat in heading south on the Garden State Parkway. He'd have me light him a cigar and I'd hand him a quarter as we approached each toll booth. Of all my memories of the shore it's the sound of the gambling wheels on the boardwalk that excites me most. These mechanized betting wheels have numbers, symbols, and words, like Mom, Pop, Lucky, and Son, painted on them. They're called "Wheels of Chance."

Standing in front of a long counter, you would place your quarter on the corresponding word, number or symbol that was painted on it. In front of you was a small little metal push button; once the button was depressed the giant pointer mounted to the center of the wheel would start spinning. Then, when you felt the moment was right, you would depress the little button again to stop the motor and if the pointer landed on your word, number or symbol, you won! If not, your quarter, along with all the others, was swept down to the end of the counter where they all fell through a slot and clanked into the metal container hidden underneath. It's the sound of the pointer spinning and picking up speed that I miss. A zwirling sound, made by the combination of the motor propelling it and the clicking of its little rubber tip as it brushed along the metal posts that lined the circumference of the wheel. Just thinking of that zwirling sound awakens a feeling of expectancy and excitement. Living in California, I miss that sound.

Recently, while on a trip back to New Jersey with my wife, Lori, I brought along my video camera to capture that sound. My plan was to mix it with music when I got back to Los Angeles. We went to Pt. Pleasant. I chose Pt. Pleasant because it was the place where I spent the greatest summer of my childhood. I was thirteen when my father left me in the hands of his bachelor buddy Willie, who owned and operated a couple of stands on the boardwalk, which included one with a wheel. My dad would come down on weekends to see how I was doing when he could. I earned my keep working the stands and cleaning up the house for Willie and the rest of his buddies who dropped in during the summer. Very soon I was trusted to run the stands, mainly because Willie would rather have fun drinking at the Rip Tide V.I.P. Room during the day than worry about the business. I admired him for that. It was the first time in my life that I was truly on my own and responsible for adult things. I was treated like one of the gang. It was as if these guys didn't even notice I was only thirteen. Now I was excited to show it all off to Lori and since I had no pictures from my past, I was happy she brought her camera.

To get the audio I wanted I intentionally picked a wheel that no one was playing and where the odds were stacked against me. There must have been over 1000 words, symbols and numbers on this wheel. You see, the odds all depended on the size of the gift. Some wheels only had four items on them, much better odds, but the gifts were much cheaper and the wheel didn't spin as fast or for as long. The stand I chose had tremendous odds because the gifts were top of the line battery—propelled scooters. For me winning wasn't a consideration, getting the loudest and longest audio recording that best represented what I recalled was my goal. Because I felt uncomfortable asking the teenage girl running the stand to spin the wheel just so I could record the sound, I decided to pay to play. So I placed my video camera on the counter, put my money down to play (now a dollar), pressed the record button on the camera and then the little metal button on the counter. The sound of the wheel zwirling around and around was as incredible as I remembered; starting slowly, picking up speed, really spinning and then after I depressed the button again winded down slowly to a stop. What the? It stopped on my symbol. A blue club. I couldn't believe it. The girl at the stand was wearing a headset microphone and broadcasted loudly through a PA system, "We have a winner! The first lucky winner of the day!" I remembered doing the same when someone would win, only back then we shouted without a PA system. Right at that moment Lori, who had been off on her own taking photos, walked up oblivious to my good fortune. I told her, "I won!"

Caught up in the excitement while looking over the prizes I asked her what I should get? This seemed a little strange because I knew that had no use for a motorized scooter. So still excited, I shifted gears and asked her who should we give one to? Having no children of our own, we started going through the list of our nephews and nieces, carefully considering who deserved such a tremendous gift and who didn't and why.

Meanwhile, a young boy about thirteen years old, walked up and began asking the girl with the headset questions. He was holding a dollar in his hand. I could tell he was deciding whether or not to play.

"Does anybody win?" he asked.

Unfortunately for him I was standing right there. She pointed at me, "He just won."

When he asked me how many tries it took? I told the truth, that is was my first try. Which didn't feel good because I knew it would just encourage him to play and most likely lose his dollar. Then he asked what prize I was going to pick and I let him know I wasn't sure yet.

He continued to tell me that if he won he would pick the electric scooter because he had one just like it, but his mom ran over it. Lori was standing between us with her back to him and facing me. She started signaling me. You know, like wives do when they want to tell you something extremely important and urgent that they don't want anyone else to know.

"Give it to him, give it to him," she was whispering and signaling.

I was in that in-between state of talking with the boy while trying to make sense of her signals. This is point when it becomes obvious to everyone around that my wife is signaling me, which makes her mad.

"Really?" I said.

"Yes!" she said, like I was a bozo, which I can be more often than not, "Who are we going to give it to? He'll love it."

I asked the boy, "Which one would you pick?"

"I'd get the black one," he said.

I turned to the girl working the stand and said, "Give him the black one."

The boy was oblivious to what I was doing because he was telling Lori the details of how his mom ran over his scooter. That's when the girl broke in to hand him the brand new one. He was in shock. He asked me why I didn't want it and told me that I could have a lot of fun with it. I let him know that because of my age he would have way more fun with it than me. He even offered me the dollar he was holding because he knew that is how much it cost me to play. I declined.

"Thanks. Wow!" he said.

I watched him walk away and Lori said, "You just made his summer!"

"There are givers and there are takers in the world, and the givers are the ones having all the fun."
- Unknown

I DEFENDED US
FROM THE BLACK MAFIA
AND ENJOYED A NIGHT AT THE THEATER

My father raised us as a single parent from the time I was nine and my brother five. He got by with some help from his buddies. Since my father worked days selling business machines for The Burroughs Corporation he had his friend, a nightclub bouncer named Paulie watch us during that time. Paulie would arrive at dawn after the end of his shift. That way there would be an adult in the house, albeit sleeping, during the first half of the day while my little brother was home alone. Eric was in kindergarten and attended the afternoon session. At noon I'd walk home from school for lunch, wake up Paulie and make Dinty Moore Beef Stew from a can for the three of us. Then after we ate I'd walk Eric to school.

Our father's parenting skills were New Jersey Zen. "Think positive, you miserable fuck." and "You're smarter than that, you fucking idiot." were just a few of his many words of encouragement.

In my effort to become more of what seemed to be a man in my father's eyes, I started lifting weights. One night the three of us were eating dinner at the kitchen table when our dad stopped eating and just stared at me.

"What?" I said with my mouth still full of food.

"Ever since you started lifting those weights you look more and more like a fucking monkey. Straighten your arms out when they're at your sides. At least make an attempt to appear human."

Disgusted, he went back to eating. Honestly, I thought I was supposed to hold my arms out from my body a little bent so that it was obvious to everyone else that I worked out. I thought the girls liked that. Ironically, my working out was the reason my dad wanted me to go to work with him one Saturday afternoon.

"Hey, let's go. You're coming to work with me." My dad said. He was dressed in his suit, tie, overcoat, hat, and was carrying his briefcase.

Before leaving the house he opened the front closet and grabbed our softball bat. I followed him out to the car. He opened up the trunk, placed his brief-case in it, and tossed in the softball bat. With his hand on the trunk about to close it, he stopped and asked, "What the fuck is that? Does that fucking thing make you smarter?" He paused for a mo-ment, "Take that fucking thing off before I knock it off!"

I took off my 'Loverboy' headband and got in the car. We drove onto Route 3 eastbound to New York

City and then up into Harlem. It was a weekend in the fall. Traffic was light as we cruised up Third Avenue. It was one of those wonderful days at summer's end when the weather is how I wished it could be forever. The sky was clear blue with puffy white clouds and the air was crisp and cool. The warmth of the sun on my skin was just right, I could enjoy it all day without breaking a sweat.

"New York is beautiful on the weekends isn't it?" he said right before taking a puff from his cigar as he drove with the windows down in his brand new Oldsmobile Cutlass Supreme Brougham. It was white with a light blue landau top and matching light blue velour interior.

He turned left down a one-way street going west. The street was lined with brownstones and we parked on the south side of the street in front of the only brownstone that had been painted. It was obvious that it was a church because it was painted white with a plexiglass encased church sign in front. The familiar church sign, with the black felt backing and the crooked white plastic letters, announcing the upcoming sermon. When my dad got out of the car so did I. I followed him to the back of his Cutlass. He unlocked the trunk, opened it up, took out his briefcase, handed me the bat and closed the trunk.

"Keep an eye on the car while I'm inside. Alright?" That was the last thing he said to me before turning around and walking up the stairs and into the church.

So there I was all alone holding a bat in the middle of Harlem. I was wearing a sleeveless teal blue muscle beach T-shirt and a pair of white corduroy Sasson jeans that were so tight I had to lie down and shimmy my way into them. Standing on the corner looking in my direction was a huge black guy. He also had a bat. Are we going to have to fight? Then the he waived at me. Just like that he held up his bat with a smile, like we were friends. Relieved I waved back holding up my bat with a smile just like he had. Now calm I realized what he was doing on the corner with a bat. It looked to me like his job was to make sure that the kid delivering groceries into the corner store wouldn't be screwed with. OK, I get it, that's how they do things around here . . . with bats.

Three more black guys were now headed toward me. They were dressed just like my dad, in suits and overcoats, wearing hats. This was unnerving because they looked like those dangerous Malcolm X types. Just as I felt my panic rise, the three of them nodded and tipped their hats to me. I nodded back and they continued on.

After what felt like an hour I got bored, so I opened the trunk, threw in the bat, and left the car to go to the corner store. I walked into the store and bought myself some candy and a copy of the Daily News. Walking out I thought to myself, "How do you like that? Even the black guy in the candy store was nice to me."

When I got back to the car, I sat in the passenger seat and read the paper while I waited for my dad.

Finally, my father returned and plopped down behind the wheel. "So, any problems?"

"No, Dad. We are parked in front of a church."

"Church? What church? That's the Black Mafia," he said.

I knew it was one of those times when you don't ask stupid questions, but I did anyway.

"Dad, what are you doing with the Black Mafia?"

"What do I do for a living?" He asked.

I answered, "Sell computers?" I was confused.

True, that's what he did; he was a representative for Burroughs Business Machines, a.k.a. computers. Keep in mind, in 1976 the smallest computer was the size of our refrigerator. My mind began to race, attempting to make sense of it all. First, you have the Mafia: OK, let's see, lopped off horses heads in the bed and short Italian guys in suits with machine guns in violin cases. Then you add 'Black.' I'm thinking about those tall skinny black dudes with huge Afros in lime green leisure suits and bell-bottoms, wearing big fancy hats with the ostrich plume, adept at ass-kicking kung fu.

Boring refrigerator-sized computers didn't seem to fit in with any of it.

"What's the Black Mafia going to do with computers?" I asked.

"Do you realize if you had just half a brain you'd be dangerous? How do you expect them to run their numbers, on their fucking fingers?" That was his answer. He had me light him a cigar for the ride home and it was never brought up again.

A few weeks later, my father wanted me to go out with him again. It was a Saturday evening when he called out to me. "Darrell, come on, we're going out tonight."

I hurried to his bedroom where he was getting dressed. Once I got there and stood in the doorway he stopped tying his tie and looked at me. "Jesus Christ, Darrell, do you own anything with a sleeve on it?"

After putting on a decent dress shirt we got in the car and once again headed east on Route 3 through the Lincoln Tunnel and into New York City. This time we drove down Broadway. New York City in the evening resembles nothing like itself during the day. At night, the lights in Times Square ignited the deep indigo blue atmosphere with bright pulsating neon. Well-dressed people flowed like a river along the wide sidewalks.

We turned west on one of the side streets and pulled up to a theater. People dressed up like famous actors I'd seen in magazines were gathered on the well-lit sidewalk chatting and smoking cigarettes. They looked happy standing underneath an illuminated marquee. The marquee lit up big red letters spelling out, *GiGi, The Musical.* We got out of the car and my father gave his keys to a man dressed in a white shirt, black slacks, and vest. Who in turn gave my dad a ticket stub and drove off with our car. My dad handed me a ticket to the performance and together we joined the crowd of beautiful people. I had never been to a Broadway show. I was fascinated, up until this moment, I had no idea that my dad had any interest at all in this sort of thing. He told me everything he felt I needed to know about the theater that night, it was obvious that this was something he really enjoyed.

I followed him all the way down to the edge of the stage where he pointed out the live musicians in the orchestra pit. After listening to them warming up for a few moments I followed him back several rows to our seats. As we took our seats he said, "This is the orchestra section. It costs a little more, but it's worth it. You'll see."

I got my first *Playbill.*

"It's just like the program at a ball game." He ran his finger down the page listing the cast and explained, "This is the starting line up, and these are the positions they play." Then he noticed a sliver of white paper tucked in his playbill with something typed on it. "I don't believe this. Agnes Morehead's part is being played by an understudy."

"Who's Agnes Morehead, Dad?"

"You know, she's the broad who plays the mother on that show, you know, *Bewitched*."

"Oh. What's an understudy?"

"Somebody else," he said.

The lights dimmed and the show began. At intermission, I followed my dad outside. He was just a few steps ahead of me when he stopped. He stood right on the edge of the sidewalk at the curb along side a lamppost and lit a cigar. I just watched him. Everyone was moving around me and chatting enthusiastically about the performance and I just stood there watching my father near the curb. I can honestly say that I don't remember a damn thing about *GiGi*, but that was the best Broadway show I've ever been to. For that one night, it felt like my dad and I were friends.

At the end of the evening, as we stood on the sidewalk waiting for the car, my dad asked, "So Darrell, what did you think? Did you have a good time?"

"Yeah, Dad I loved it. It was great."

"Yeah, well it really wasn't the best show for your first show." He went on, "You know what? I'll tell you what. Why don't we start a new tradition?

Every year you, me, and that silly little son-of-a-bitch you call your brother, will go to a play. Would you like that?"

"Yeah, Dad. That'd be great."

It was a promise he kept until he died five years later. The last year of his life he was too sick to attend, but had tickets for Eric and I. I was eighteen, so I drove the two of us into New York City to see *The Best Little Whorehouse in Texas*.

When we got home we both went straight to our bed-ridden father who enthusiastically asked us, "So what did you think? Was it good? Did you have a good time?"

Eric and I both went on to tell him how great the seats were, how I gave the car to the valet just like he had when he drove us, and how surprising it was when the Sheriff in the play fired his gun on stage. He lay there smiling as we enthusiastically rambled on about how well our evening went without him.

I just like wearing the costume. I had no idea I was supposed to have a mission.

STING PREVENTS
WORLD WAR III

When I was child I was terrified of flying. I had never been on a plane, nor were there any plans for me to be on a plane—but I dreaded the thought. When my father returned from a business trip to California, I asked him about his flight.

"Weren't you afraid of the plane crashing?"

"Darrell," he answered, "the pilots don't want to crash either."

My father's casual and confident response, transformed my outlook. I remember thinking, "He's right." I never thought about it like that before. If the pilots don't want to crash either they'll do everything in their power to make sure we don't. My father's simple response had the power to radically transformed my life, by eliminating my fear of flying.

During the late eighties I was serving in the U.S. Coast Guard. It was the height of the Cold War and I had just finished a tour aboard the USCGC *Jarvis* patrolling the Bering Sea. Our mission was to monitor suspicious Soviet ships that we assumed were spying on the U.S. These were tense times. We believed we were under the constant threat of a nuclear attack by the Russians. It felt like my comrades and I were sitting on a ticking time bomb that would go off at any moment sending us to the front lines and certain death.

Then I heard a song on the radio. One line of that song radically transformed how I felt. It was a line in the chorus that went, "If the Russians love their children, too." My reaction was incredibly similar to that of my father's idea of air travel, and its effect was just as profound. The song was titled "Russians," performed by Sting.

I thought, "He's right!" If the Russians love their children, too, then they don't want war either. This simple truth transformed the Russians from an army of anonymous American haters to vulnerable people just like us. No longer having to defend against hate, I felt compassion.

After having this realization, thanks to Sting, I decided to cooperate with it. I purchased a beach ball that was a globe of the earth. Each morning as I sat on my balcony to do my morning meditation I'd hug the globe and imagine love going around the world. In my mind's eye I'd see Russian families smiling lovingly with their children. I'd also do visualize the same with American families. As I continued this practice I didn't restrict it to just Americans and Soviets. If there was any news of hostile situations in other parts of the world, I'd imagine the same loving thoughts about those people with their families as well.

At the beginning of 1989, indication of an eminent Soviet/American nuclear strike escalated throughout the branches of the military. My prayers seemed to be working because I no longer felt disturbed by this. Deep down I felt there was no threat. At this time I was working as a special liaison with members of all five branches of the military. One day a co-worker, a U.S. Marine Corps Staff Sergeant confided, "Aren't you worried we'll be at war soon?"

"No, the Russians don't want to go to war either," I answered.

"Really? I never thought about it like that before." He grinned and was relieved as we proceeded with our day's assignment. Before the year's end, news of the fall of the Berlin Wall made headlines around the world. It's truly amazing how just one idea, one little thought, can transform your life.

"Divine Love is the most powerful chemical in the universe, and dissolves everything which is not of itself!"
- Florence Scovel Shinn

THE END